W9-AHI-706

Witness History Series

BLITZKRIEG!

Peter Chrisp

The Bookwright Press
New York • 1991

Titles in this series

Cover illustration: A Nazi propaganda poster, with advancing German tanks beneath the Swastika.

First published in the United States in 1991 by
The Bookwright Press
387 Park Avenue South
New York, NY 10016

First published in 1990 by
Wayland (Publishers) Ltd
61 Western Road, Hove
East Sussex BN3 1JD, England

Library of Congress Cataloging-in-Publication Data
Chrisp. Peter.
    Blitzkrieg / by Peter Chrisp.
    p. cm. – (Witness history)
    Includes bibliographical references and index.
    Summary: Surveys German military strategy
    during World War II.
    ISBN 0-531-18373-4
    1. World War, 1939-1945– Campaigns–Juvenile
    literature. 2. World War,
    1939-1945–Germany–Juvenile literature. 3.
    Germany–History–1933-1945–Juvenile literature.
    [1. World War, 1939-1945–Campaigns. 2. World
    War, 1939-1945–Germany. 3.
    Germany–History–1933-1945.] I. Title. II. Series:
    Witness history series.   90-42856
    D743.C454 1991   CIP
    940.54'213–dc20   AC

Typeset by Rachel Gibbs, Wayland
Printed in Italy by G.Canale & C.S.p.A., Turin

Contents

1
INTRODUCTION
The lessons of trench warfare

ON SEPTEMBER 1, 1939, Germany's armed forces invaded Poland. The attack opened with surprise bombing raids on Poland's railroad system and airfields. Then tanks and motorized columns swept across the borders in pincer movements, encircling the Polish armies. Overwhelmed by the speed of the invasion, Poland was unable to coordinate its defenses; it was conquered in less than a month. The following May, the same pattern of events was repeated when the German Army overran the Netherlands, Belgium and France. By the summer of 1940, Germany had conquered a new European empire stretching from the French Atlantic coast to the west of Poland.

This was blitzkrieg, or "lightning war," a revolutionary new form of warfare. Partly psychological, it was designed to defeat an enemy not by destroying its forces but by paralyzing them. Like lightning, blitzkrieg was swift and unexpected – its success depended on speed and surprise.

Blitzkrieg tactics developed as a reaction against the stalemate of trench warfare. World War I (1914–18) had begun with a short period of mobile fighting, when Germany had invaded Belgium and France.

An early British tank. At first the tanks were used in small numbers to support the infantry. It was not until they were used in large numbers that they showed their tactical potential.

◀ Storm-troopers training. They moved rapidly in single file, under cover of smoke. Their main weapons were hand grenades, shown in a pile on the right.

▼ Simply surviving the cramped and uncomfortable living conditions in the trenches of World War I was a test of human endurance for soldiers such as these Canadians.

But the German advance had been halted, and the rival armies – Britain and France against Germany – had dug themselves into strong defensive positions. On the Western Front they faced each other from trenches, defended by barbed wire and machine guns.

An attack would take the form of an artillery bombardment, followed by an infantry charge across "no-man's-land." Such tactics gave the defenders an enormous advantage. On the first day of the Battle of the Somme, 19, 240 British soldiers were killed as they ran toward the Germans who were alerted by the preliminary bombardment.

How could mobility be restored to the battlefield? Both Germany and Britain came up with partial solutions to the problem. The German solution was the storm-trooper. The fittest soldiers in the army, storm-troopers were used to make quick, deep penetrations behind enemy lines. They avoided strong points, jumping over trenches rather than fighting for them. Their targets were the artillery and the divisional headquarters behind the front lines.

The British solution was the tank, a machine specifically designed to cross trenches and barbed wire. It was used most effectively at the Battle of Amiens in August 1918, when four hundred tanks caused panic in the German lines with a surprise attack. However, the early tanks were unable to

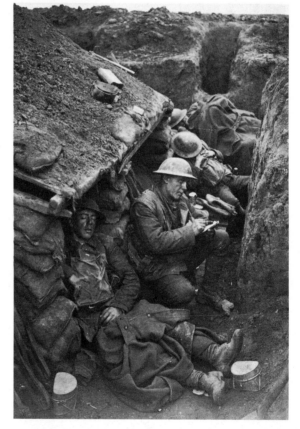

advance long distances, and the offensive ended after three days. Neither tanks nor storm-troopers had enough mobility to win a decisive victory, but they pointed the way to the methods of blitzkrieg.

The elements of blitzkrieg

An important factor in the success of blitzkrieg tactics was the use of wireless communication between tanks. This is a Panzer IV, the mainstay of the panzer divisions for the first part of World War II.

In the 1920s and 1930s, improvements in technology gave the German Army the mobility the storm-troopers had lacked. Most important was efficient motorization in the form of reliable tanks and support vehicles. Improvements in radio communication meant that the new fast-moving armies could receive fresh orders throughout a battle. The third vital development was that of air power. A new type of plane called a Stuka provided Germany with a form of flying artillery – the dive-bomber could bombard enemy targets accurately. These technological changes made the development of blitzkrieg possible.

Blitzkrieg combined a number of important elements:

- **Surprise**: The object of a blitzkrieg attack was the paralysis of the enemy's defenses – the enemy had to be caught off guard in a surprise attack. Hitler reversed the conventional order of events by invading a country and then declaring war.
- **Psychological warfare**: Used to heighten the sense of surprise and cause confusion.

Before an attack, the Germans would use propaganda to weaken the enemy's will to fight. During an attack, screeching sirens on the Stukas caused terror. Germany also used parachutists, dropped behind the enemy lines to create chaos. Methods of deception, such as dummy tanks and dummy parachutists, were used to mislead the enemy.

- **Concentration of firepower**: To ensure an initial breakthrough, the Germans concentrated their firepower on a narrow front. The object was always the weakest defended section of the enemy lines where least resistance would be encountered.
- **Speed**: In 1937, Heinz Guderian, the creator of the German Army's panzer divisions, wrote:

Everything. . . is dependent on this: to be able to move faster than has hitherto been done, to keep moving despite the enemy's defensive fire and thus to make it harder for him to build up fresh defensive positions, and finally to carry the attack deep into the enemy's defenses.[1]

- **Leadership from the front**: To avoid strongly defended points and maintain the momentum of the attack, improvisation was essential. According to General von Thoma, "the tactical task for the commander is up front."[2] Unlike the First World War generals, who issued orders from headquarters miles behind the lines, von Thoma and Guderian drove into battle with their panzers. They could then quickly amend orders to adapt to new circumstances.
- **Coordination**: Major-General Mellenthin wrote that "a German panzer division was a highly flexible formation of all arms."[3] These included reconnaissance aircraft, artillery and motorized infantry, all working in close cooperation. By coordinating the different forces in this way, the Germans could maximize the effect of an attack.

Many of these elements derived from the lessons of trench warfare. But of all the nations fighting in World War I, only Germany developed blitzkrieg tactics. To understand why, we must look at the history of the European powers between the wars.

The dive-bombing Stuka was designed specifically for surprise attacks. However, because they were poorly armed and slow, Stukas were vulnerable to enemy attack.

THE FIRST WORLD WAR ended in November 1918 when Germany's leaders sued for peace. Germany itself was not invaded by the Allies, but after years of naval blockade its people were desperately short of food, clothing and fuel. Their morale received a devastating blow when the United States entered the war – by July 1918, 250,000 American troops were arriving in France each month. In November 1918, the German Navy in Kiel mutinied. This was followed by a wave of strikes throughout Germany calling for peace. To avoid revolution, Germany's leaders were forced to end the war.

In 1919, the victorious Allies met at Versailles to draw up a peace treaty, which Germany was then forced to sign. To most Germans, this treaty was deeply humiliating. They were blamed for having started the war and forced to pay huge reparations. Germany's armed forces were drastically reduced and forbidden to enter the Rhineland. Germany also lost large areas of territory to neighboring countries.

The world economic depression of 1929 created massive unemployment in Germany. When a succession of democratic governments were unable to solve the country's problems, more and more people were attracted by the solutions offered by the extremist parties – the Communist Party and the Nazi Party of Adolf Hitler. Much of Hitler's appeal came from his promise to tear up the Treaty of Versailles. The Nazis, he said,

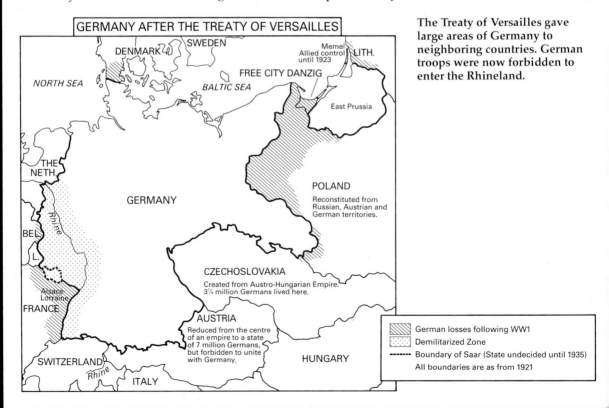

GERMANY AFTER THE TREATY OF VERSAILLES

DENMARK

SWEDEN

Memel
Allied control
until 1923

LITH.

NORTH SEA

FREE CITY DANZIG

BALTIC SEA

East Prussia

THE NETH.

POLAND
Reconstituted from
Russian, Austrian and
German territories.

GERMANY

Rhine

BEL.

L.

CZECHOSLOVAKIA
Created from Austro-Hungarian Empire.
3¼ million Germans lived here.

Alsace
Lorraine

FRANCE

AUSTRIA
Reduced from the centre
of an empire to a state
of 7 million Germans,
but forbidden to unite
with Germany.

SWITZERLAND

Rhine

ITALY

HUNGARY

▨ German losses following WW1
▦ Demilitarized Zone
------ Boundary of Saar (State undecided until 1935)
All boundaries are as from 1921

The Treaty of Versailles gave large areas of Germany to neighboring countries. German troops were now forbidden to enter the Rhineland.

would wipe out Germany's humiliation and bring about a national revival. At the end of January 1933, Hitler was appointed Chancellor of Germany.

Long before Hitler came to power, the German Army had been trying secretly to avoid the restrictions imposed at Versailles. To curb German military power, the Treaty of Versailles had limited the army to 100,000 men, but these soldiers were trained to form the core of a much larger force. Under Hitler's leadership, this illicit army rapidly expanded.

It was inevitable that this army would try to develop new military strategies. The old methods had failed Germany in 1918, but they were in any case irrelevant to a small professional army. What kind of tactics could such a force adopt?

When the Germans failed to pay reparations at the end of 1922, the French sent troops into the industrial Ruhr to take what was owed by force. This was another humiliation for Germany, and the occupation of the Ruhr was a source of great bitterness towards the French.

One way to compensate for an army's smallness is to increase its mobility. General von Seeckt, Commander-in-Chief in the 1920s, wrote that the future of warfare lay "in the employment of mobile armies, relatively small, but of high quality."[4] The next step was taken by a young officer, Heinz Guderian, who argued that wars could be won by the use of tanks. In 1933, at a display of experimental tanks organized by Guderian, Hitler cried: "That's what I need! That's what I want to have!"[5]

France and Britain

Many people were determined to prevent another world war. In May 1936, thousands gathered in Trafalgar Square for a great peace rally. Paper gas masks recall the horrors of World War I.

Although the French and British were the victors in 1918, they had little reason to celebrate. The price of victory had been the deaths of millions of men on the Western Front. In France, where the birth-rate had been falling even before the war, the impact was terrible: postwar France seemed almost a nation of old people. Much of the fighting had taken place on French territory, and some of the richest industrial areas had been devastated. Britain's losses had not been as great, but the horror of trench warfare would not be forgotten.

In both countries there was a general revulsion against the senselessness and waste of war. People believed that the war had been fought "to end all wars." In future, it was hoped, international disputes would be settled peacefully by the newly created League of Nations. There was a strong reaction against militarism and great pressure for disarmament.

In Britain, the result was a big cut-back in military spending. In 1919, the army was told to assume there would be no major war for ten years, and to plan accordingly. It was to be responsible for home security and the defense of the Empire, but there would be no future need to send forces to the Continent.

There was a great resistance within the army to the development of tanks and this was reinforced by the development of anti-tank weapons. In 1932 Sir James Edmonds, an official war historian, wrote, "any tank which shows its nose will, in my opinion, be knocked out at once."[6]

French military thinking was still dominated by the tactics of World War I, in particular the belief in the defensive. Defensive tactics also suited the French people's disillusionment with war. Marshal Pétain, the Commander-in-Chief, had successfully organized the defense of Verdun against the biggest German offensive of the whole war. His success had been partly due to the use of underground forts, which had withstood the heaviest German bombardment. This principle was now used in the construction of the Maginot Line – a permanent system of fortifications that was built along the German border. Toward the end of his life Pétain said:

After the war of 1914–18, it was finished for me. My military mind was closed. When I saw the introduction of other tools, other methods, I must say they didn't interest me.[7]

Pétain's experience during World War I had apparently closed his mind to new methods.

"The Harvest of Battle," by the English painter C.R.W. Nevinson represented the feelings of many British people after 1918.

The USSR

At the end of World War I, Russia was an international outcast. The Revolution of 1917 had brought to power the Communist government of Lenin's Bolshevik Party. Russia had been fighting alongside France and Britain, but after the Revolution the Bolsheviks had made a separate peace with Germany. The Allies had responded by sending troops to Russia, in an effort to topple the Bolsheviks and restore an eastern front. Even after the war ended, Allied troops continued to fight in Russia, supporting the anti-communist White Armies in the civil war. But Lenin's regime survived, and the Bolsheviks called upon the working classes in western Europe to follow their example and stage a revolution. The political leaders of Germany, France and Britain were all afraid that revolution might spread to their own countries.

After Lenin's death, the new USSR came increasingly under the control of a dictator, Joseph Stalin. He was not interested in world revolution, calling instead for "Socialism in One Country." Encircled by capitalist states, Stalin believed the USSR had to become a strong industrial nation as quickly as possible.

The Red Army's greatest military strategist was Marshal Mikhail Tukhachevsky. Like Guderian, he stressed the importance of the offensive and the use of mobility.

In the 1930s, Joseph Stalin was proclaimed by the Soviet people as the father and protector of the USSR, but his 1937 purge of the officer corps weakened the Red Army. The USSR's lack of experienced officers was later an important factor in encouraging Hitler's military ambitions.

During the Spanish Civil War of 1936, the USSR supplied the Republicans with many tanks. Although these were never used in a concentrated mass, the Republican defeat helped convince Stalin that Tukhachevsky's ideas were wrong.

Tukhachevsky argued for the deployment of massive numbers of tanks in close cooperation with airplanes, artillery and motorized infantry. Early in 1937, he wrote:

> *As for the blitzkrieg which is so propagandized by the Germans, this is directed towards an enemy who doesn't want to and won't fight it out. If the Germans meet an opponent who stands up and fights and takes the offensive himself, that would give a different aspect to things.* [8]

This differed substantially from the French defensive approach.

Six months later, Tukhachevsky was dead, shot for treason on Stalin's orders. In order to consolidate his power, Stalin had launched a ruthless purge of the Red Army. In the following months, 35,000 men – half of the Soviet officer corps – were shot or imprisoned.

After the military purge, the Red Army was dominated by old-fashioned cavalry officers, men like Budenny and Voroshilov. The only marshals to survive the purge, they both owed their position to friendship with Stalin. Neither understood modern warfare. As a result, the mechanized formations that Tukhachevsky had created were broken up, and the tanks dispersed for infantry support in the French manner. The Red Army seemed to have been crippled.

13

3
STEPS TO WAR
German expansion 1936–9

THE YEARS 1936–9 WERE a period of great German expansion. In March 1936, Hitler ordered his troops to enter the Rhineland. This was a direct challenge to France, but Hitler guessed the French would do nothing to resist.

Hitler's next move, in March 1938, was directed against German-speaking Austria. Following a campaign of threats against the Austrian government, the German Army marched into Vienna, and Hitler proclaimed the "Anschluss," or union, between Germany and Austria.

Czechoslovakia was Hitler's next objective. Over three million German-speakers lived there, in the Sudetenland.

Hitler claimed that they were an oppressed minority and made increasing demands of the Czech government. Czechoslovakia had a strong army and an alliance with France. If Germany invaded, the French would be obliged to come to the aid of the Czechs: the result could be a European war. But after reaching an agreement with Hitler at the Munich Conference of September 1938, the French and British forced Czechoslovakia to surrender the Sudetenland without a fight.

David Low's cartoon, which appeared in the British newspaper the *Evening Standard* on February 17, 1936, shows a campaign of increasing German pressure on Austria.

INCREASING PRESSURE.

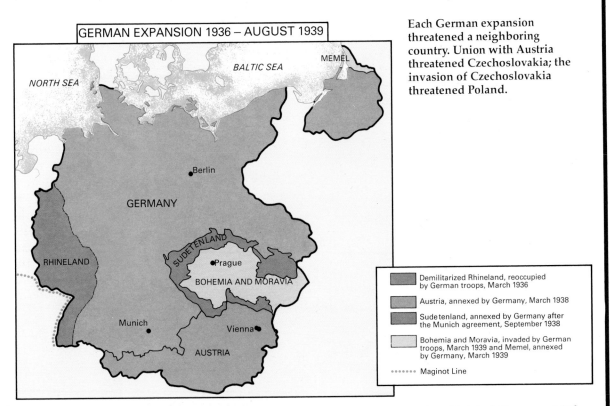

GERMAN EXPANSION 1936 – AUGUST 1939

NORTH SEA

BALTIC SEA

MEMEL

Berlin

GERMANY

RHINELAND

SUDETENLAND

Prague

BOHEMIA AND MORAVIA

Munich

Vienna

AUSTRIA

Demilitarized Rhineland, reoccupied by German troops, March 1936

Austria, annexed by Germany, March 1938

Sudetenland, annexed by Germany after the Munich agreement, September 1938

Bohemia and Moravia, invaded by German troops, March 1939 and Memel, annexed by Germany, March 1939

••••••• Maginot Line

Each German expansion threatened a neighboring country. Union with Austria threatened Czechoslovakia; the invasion of Czechoslovakia threatened Poland.

Hitler promised that this was his last demand, but six months later Germany occupied the rest of Czechoslovakia.

Why were the European powers unable to prevent German expansion? The League of Nations' ability to prevent aggression depended on the willingness of its member countries to use force. But in the 1930s, France and Britain were desperate to avoid war. Hitler's demand for a united Germany seemed reasonable, so British and French leaders followed a policy of appeasement.

Appeasement ended in March 1939 when Hitler destroyed the Czech state. Britain and France determined to resist further aggression. In April, the British gave a military guarantee to Poland, Hitler's next likely target. This was designed to deter Hitler – but after Munich, how seriously would he take this guarantee?

In 1938, Winston Churchill described Hitler's policy as a "program of aggression... unfolding stage by stage."[9] Others claimed that Hitler was an opportunist, who exploited

the weaknesses of a divided Europe. Hitler himself expressed both views:

> *The politically fluid world situation ... demands constant preparedness for war ... to make possible the military exploitation of politically favorable opportunities should they occur.*[10]

> *All the individual decisions that have been realized since 1933 are not the result of momentary considerations, but represent the implementation of a previously existing plan, though perhaps not exactly according to the schedule that was envisaged.*[11]

The first quotation comes from a military directive of July 1937, the second from a secret speech Hitler gave his generals in February 1939. Hitler's approach to warfare was both practical and aggressive.

Hitler's war aims

In his book *Mein Kampf*, published in 1925, Adolf Hitler argued that Germany lacked *Lebensraum*, or "living space," and urgently needed "new soil in Europe" for its growing population:

> If we speak of new soil in Europe today we can have primarily in mind only Russia and her vassal border states . . . The giant empire in the east is ripe for collapse.[12]

Russia, weakened by civil war and purge of its army, was a tempting target.

Hitler's argument for "living space" was

A British wartime propaganda poster that claimed to reveal Nazi Germany's plans for extending its empire and ruling Europe.

largely ignored, or dismissed as the ravings of a fanatic. Nevertheless, it remained his lifelong obsession. "Living space" could only be acquired in a war of conquest. But what sort of war would Germany, which was surrounded by potentially hostile countries, be capable of winning?

The type of war Germany could fight depended on its rearmament program. The German economy depended on imports for its raw materials, the supply of which was likely to be cut off in the event of war. So

Germany could either stockpile raw materials to prepare for a long war or concentrate on the production of weapons, thereby increasing the army's striking power at the start of a war. General von Thoma, the army's economics chief, described this as a choice between "armament in breadth" (weapons production) and "armament in depth" (raw materials):

> *By armament in breadth I mean the number and strength of the armed forces . . . Armament in depth, on the other hand, embraces all those measures . . . which serve to provide supplies during war and therefore strengthen our powers of endurance.[13]*

There were advantages and disadvantages to each policy.

In 1936 Hitler's own view was:

> *It would . . . be better for the nation to enter the war without a single kilogram of copper in stock but with full munitions depots rather than with empty munitions depots . . . There can be no building up of a reserve of raw materials for the event of war.[14]*

Hitler did not want a war of endurance – the type of war Germany had lost in 1918. He believed Germany could defeat its enemies only one at a time, in short, limited wars.

In April 1939, Hitler issued a directive for the first of his short wars. The enemy was to be Poland. To make certain the war did not spread, Hitler signed a non-aggression pact with Poland's eastern neighbor, the USSR, in August 1939. The last thing Hitler wanted, or expected, was another world war.

In August 1939, Germany and the USSR signed a non-aggression pact. This picture shows, from left to right: German Under-states Secretary Gaus; Soviet leader Joseph Stalin; Soviet Foreign Minister Molotov. Hitler intended to fight a short war against Poland alone. The invasion of Poland would be paid for by captured raw materials, which would help Germany in future wars.

17

4
BLITZKRIEG
Poland – blitzkrieg in practice

The political leaders consider it their task . . . to limit the war to Poland only . . . The isolation of Poland will be all the more easily maintained if we succeed in starting the war with sudden heavy blows and in gaining rapid successes.[15]

THIS EXTRACT FROM HITLER'S April 1939 war directive shows the close relationship between his diplomacy and military tactics. His primary concern in planning the war on Poland was to prevent its allies, Britain and France, from starting a simultaneous war in the west. Hitler believed he had achieved this objective with the 1939 Nazi-Soviet Pact. Without the prospect of Soviet help, he thought the Western powers would do little to defend Poland, and they would be even less likely to fight if Poland were defeated swiftly.

Geographically and strategically, Poland was the perfect target for a blitzkrieg attack. It is a flat country, and west of the broad Vistula River it offers no natural obstacles to an invasion. In the dry summer of 1939, this was ideal tank country. The Germans could launch their attack anywhere along a 1,750-mile border, in the north, south or west.

Poland had a large army, but it was hopelessly out of date, with eleven cavalry brigades but hardly any tanks. In an attempt to defend their entire border, the Poles spread their forces out in a linear fashion. This was partly a result of self-confidence and national pride. But Poland's industrial centers were all in the vulnerable south and west. If these were lost, Poland would be unable to keep its armies supplied.

In April 1939, the Polish cavalry was training close to the German borders. The German Army was not deterred by the Polish troops.

German infantry running through a burning forest during the invasion of Poland. The Germans waged a type of war the Poles had not experienced before.

On September 1, 1939, the blitzkrieg opened with surprise bombing raids on Poland's airfields. Within twenty-four hours most of Poland's air force had been destroyed. Then the bombers switched their attacks to the railroad system and military convoys, disrupting mobilization.

Meanwhile, armored divisions swept across the borders, easily breaking through the lines of defense, then driving on in great pincer movements toward Warsaw. Despite fierce resistance, the encircled Polish armies were overwhelmed by the speed of the invasion. Behind the lines, radio propaganda broadcast in Polish produced confusion and demoralization.

The final blow fell on September 17 when the USSR, anxious to seize its share of the spoils, invaded from the east. The Polish Army could offer little resistance.

It had taken Hitler less than a month to conquer Poland. However, one part of his invasion plan had gone seriously wrong. On September 3, the British and French had decided to honor their obligations to Poland and had declared war on Germany.

The Phoney War

British troops spent the "Phoney War" constructing trenches in Flanders. The Allies had not yet grasped the concept of blitzkrieg.

France and Britain entered the war to help Poland, but by the time their slowly moving armies had mobilized, the war in the east was over. They now did little but wait in their defensive positions. For the front-line soldiers this was a boring and frustrating period, nicknamed the "Phoney War." Even during this period of apparent calm, the Germans pursued the use of psychological warfare in the form of propaganda:

Why should war in the west be fought? For the restoration of Poland? It would be senseless to annihilate millions of men to reconstruct this state.[16]

Don't transform France into a vast battlefield . . . don't listen to perfidious England.[17]

Such propaganda had a predictable effect on the morale of the Allied soldiers.

French troops also experienced French anti-war propaganda, particularly from the Communist Party. Following the Soviet line, the French Communists campaigned against the war and, it was alleged, sabotaged war production. Stories of such sabotage, whether true or false, convinced many French people that Hitler had active sympathizers working within France.

Meanwhile the French generals had learned no lessons from the Polish campaign: they continued to believe in linear defense. Germany's success was put down to the inferior equipment of the Polish Army. According to General Duffieux, blitzkrieg would have no chance against the French:

> *How can these armored units hurl themselves unsupported against our lines, as in Poland, and penetrate deep into them, without risking almost complete obliteration?* [18]

General Gamelin, the Commander-in-Chief, placed his faith in the superior experience of the French commanders. The German generals were too young:

> *I can think of few of their present generals who fought in responsible posts in 1914–18. Here we are almost all former 1918 divisional commanders.* [19]

But times had changed, and it was a disadvantage that so many French generals were steeped in the outmoded traditions of World War I.

Meanwhile, the small British Expeditionary Force dug trenches around Lille, close to the Belgian border. In October 1939 the French writer, André Maurois, visited the British trenches:

> *One of [the English officers] showing me a miserable trench which his men were digging with great difficulty, said in an apologetic tone: "Obviously this would never stop a tank. But, after all, there's a thick forest in front of my battalion and it's reasonable to hope the tanks won't come this way."* [20]

The "reasonable" hope was to prove unfounded.

The turret of one of the underground fortresses in the Maginot Line, exposed by German shelling. This line was considered to be impregnable.

Operation Sicklecut

In October 1939, the German High Command developed a plan for an offensive in the west. It was to take the form of an advance through northern Belgium and a frontal attack on the Allied armies. This was the route taken by the Germans in 1914, and would have come as no surprise to the Allies.

General von Rundstedt's Chief of Staff, General von Manstein, criticized the plan and suggested a revised version:

> *Right from the start the center of gravity should be in the southern wing. By definitely transferring the center of gravity in this way, the strong enemy forces that may be expected in north Belgium will be cut off and destroyed.[21]*

◀ A German parachutist leaps from a plane during the attack on the Netherlands. Parachutists were dropped ahead of the advancing tanks to seize bridges and sabotage other targets. To create confusion, dummy parachutists were also widely scattered.

▼ The Allied forces outnumbered the German in everything except aircraft. Yet for a long time they were beaten by the German Army.

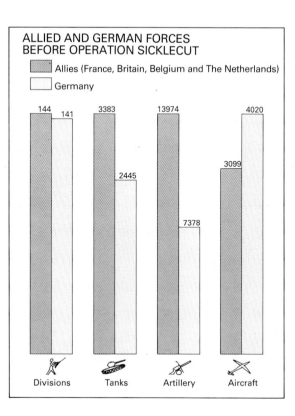

ALLIED AND GERMAN FORCES
BEFORE OPERATION SICKLECUT

Allies (France, Britain, Belgium and The Netherlands)
Germany

	Divisions	Tanks	Artillery	Aircraft
Allies	144	3383	13974	3099
Germany	141	2445	7378	4020

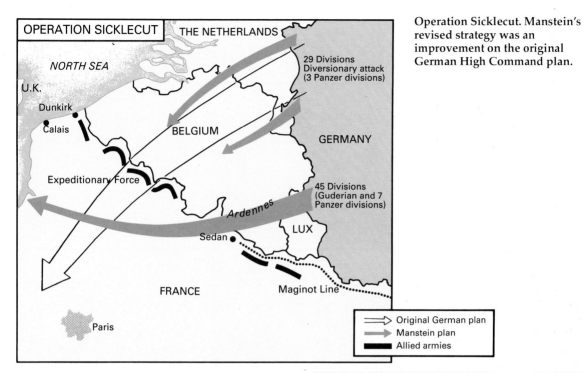

OPERATION SICKLECUT

NORTH SEA

U.K.

Dunkirk

Calais

THE NETHERLANDS

BELGIUM

Expeditionary Force

Ardennes

Sedan

FRANCE

Paris

GERMANY

29 Divisions
Diversionary attack
(3 Panzer divisions)

45 Divisions
(Guderian and 7
Panzer divisions)

LUX

Maginot Line

Original German plan
Manstein plan
Allied armies

Operation Sicklecut. Manstein's revised strategy was an improvement on the original German High Command plan.

Manstein's plan was to send the bulk of the German tanks through the wooded hills of the Ardennes, in the south of Belgium. This area was thought to be unsuitable for tanks and would be thinly defended. The attack on the northern wing would divert attention from the main thrust in the south. After breaking through the Ardennes, the tanks would sweep up behind the Allied armies like the cut of a sickle.

The High Command rejected Manstein's plan, but Hitler, who had doubts about the original version, was impressed. When a plane carrying the original plan fell into Belgian hands, "Operation Sicklecut" was immediately adopted.

On May 10, 1940, the blitzkrieg opened with airborne attacks on the Netherlands and northern Belgium – gliders and parachutists took the defenders completely by surprise. The Allies reacted by advancing into northern Belgium to meet the invasion; meanwhile the bulk of the Wehrmacht, with seven panzer divisions, broke through the thinly defended French lines at Sedan in the south. André Maurois wrote:

Victory and defeat are habits. After the disaster at Sedan the myth of the enemy's invincibility spread rapidly and served as an excuse for all those who wanted to retreat.[22]

On May 21, when the Germans had reached the Channel, Paul Reynaud, the French Premier, spoke to the Senate:

The truth is that our classic conception of war has come up against a new conception. Basic in this . . . is not only massive use of heavy armored divisions and cooperation between them and airplanes, but also the creation of disorder in the enemy's rear by parachute raids . . . We must think of the new type of warfare we are facing and take immediate decisions.[23]

The French had grasped the concept of blitzkrieg, but with their armies in full retreat, it is difficult to see what kind of "immediate decision" they could have taken.

5
BRITAIN AGAINST GERMANY
Blitz on Britain

Two German Dornier bombers photographed during an attack on South London. The intensive bombing raids did not have the effect Hitler hoped for.

ON MAY 23, 1940, GUDERIAN'S panzers were only a few miles from Dunkirk, the only possible escape route for the retreating British Expeditionary Force. To Guderian's surprise, Hitler ordered the tanks to halt. As a result, the British were able to rescue 338,000 men from Dunkirk. Why did Hitler allow the British troops to escape?

General Blumentritt recalled meeting Hitler at this time:

[Hitler] astonished us by speaking with admiration of the British Empire, of the necessity for its existence . . . He said that all he wanted from Britain was that she should acknowledge Germany's position on the Continent . . . his aim was to make peace with Britain on a basis that she would regard as honorable to accept.[24]

This might serve to explain in part why Hitler had spared the British Expeditionary Force.

After the French armistice on June 22, the British were fighting alone. But to Hitler's consternation, they refused to admit that the war was over. Reluctantly Hitler ordered preparations for a risky naval invasion – to be used only as a last resort.

For a naval invasion to have any chance of succeeding, Germany had to win control of the air. In July, the *Luftwaffe* started a campaign against Britain's airfields and aircraft factories. For more than two months, Spitfires and Messerschmitts fought a desperate battle in the skies over Britain.

On September 7, with the Royal Air Force (RAF) close to breaking point, the *Luftwaffe* unexpectedly changed its tactics and began to bomb the East End of London. The Blitz, Germany's night bombing campaign on Britain's cities, had begun.

What did Germany hope to gain by bombing civilian targets? The *Luftwaffe* was using tactics developed soon after World War I by an Italian general, Giulio Douhet. He wrote:

> *A complete breakdown of the social structure cannot but take place in a country subjected to this kind of merciless pounding from the air . . . the people themselves, driven by the instinct of self-preservation, would rise up and demand an end to war.*[25]

The campaign was partly psychological in character, designed to destroy the British will to fight. Hitler hoped to make Britain ask for peace without the need for a costly invasion.

In spite of massive destruction, the bombing failed in its objectives. There was not a "complete breakdown of the social structure." The very regularity of the raids allowed many Londoners to adapt to the bombing. Douhet's theory about bombing civilian targets turned out to be unreliable.

In May 1941, when there was still no British peace proposal, Hitler called off the bombing. He needed the *Luftwaffe* for a new campaign: the invasion of the USSR.

In October 1941, the area around London's St. Paul's Cathedral was devastated by German bombing.

The blitzkrieg economy

This extract from the postwar memoirs of Albert Speer, Germany's minister of armaments, refers to the short-lived German Revolution of 1918. This had been a reaction against a prolonged and unpopular war. Hitler's fear of revolution made him cautious about imposing strict economic measures at home.

It seemed to many Germans in the summer of 1940 that their economy had been scarcely

A March 1940 poster asking Germans to give money to help the war effort. Despite such campaigns, in 1940 German consumers were barely affected by the cost of the war.

26

affected by the war. No attempt was made to reduce the use of labor in non-essential industries, nor to conscript women into war work. Large sums of money were spent on public works, such as superhighways and impressive public buildings. Between 1940 and 1941, the production of consumer goods increased in volume. At the same time, armaments production was actually cut back.

The thriving German economy was due to the exploitation of the conquered territories. These were expected to pay for the costs of the German occupation, fixed far in excess of real costs: in 1940, France paid 1.75 billion Reichsmarks; in 1941, 5.55 billion. They were also expected to provide raw materials for the German war machine. This chart shows the percentage of French production taken by Germany during the occupation.[27]

Coal	29%	Iron ore	74%
Petroleum/motor fuel	80%	Steel products	51%
Copper	75%	Aluminum	75%
Lead	43%	Rubber	38%
Magnesium	100%	Platinum	76%

This drain of raw materials meant a lowered standard of living in France, and also offered a blow to national pride.

One of the greatest benefits for Germany was the use of foreign labor, which released German workers for the armed forces. These statistics show the extent of foreign workers in the German war economy.[28]

	1939	1940	1941
Germans	39,114,000	35,239,000	34,528,000
Foreign civilians	301,000	803,000	1,753,000
Prisoners of war	—	348,000	1,316,000
Total foreigners	301,000	1,151,000	3,069,000
Foreigners as % of all employees	0.8%	3.2%	8.5%

Between the summer of 1940 and the autumn of 1941, Hitler was at the peak of his popularity. The blitzkrieg strategy had succeeded beyond anyone's expectations. Most Germans believed the war was over.

German troops gathering for their triumphal march through Paris in 1940.

This cartoon from the British newspaper the *Daily Mail*, April 15, 1941, shows the Arabs in the foreground baffled by a European war fought across their territory. The cartoonist compares the desert war to an endless merry-go-round.

SOON AFTER THE GERMAN conquest of France, the war spread to a new area of operations – the desert of North Africa. Here the British first learned to use a blitzkrieg attack. With both sides using mobile offensive tactics, the result was a rapidly changing war of movement: between September 1940 and May 1943, the same stretch of Libyan coastline changed hands five times as first one side, then the other, gained the advantage.

The desert war was started by Mussolini, the Italian dictator, whose ambition was to create an Italian Empire in the Mediterranean. Britain and France, each controlling parts of North Africa, stood in his way, but their defeat in 1940 provided Mussolini with his opportunity. In September 1940, he ordered his army in Libya to invade Egypt, held by a much smaller British force.

Mussolini's was an old-fashioned infantry army, with few tanks and no understanding of mobile warfare. After advancing fifty miles it stopped at Sidi Barrani, and built a chain of defensive camps. Major-General O'Connor, in charge of the smaller but more mobile British forces, saw the opportunity to use a blitzkrieg attack. Early on December 9, the British tanks found a gap in the Italian defenses and made a surprise attack behind the lines. The result was devastating: one by one the Italian camps surrendered. O'Connor followed up his victory with a rapid drive into Libya. Within two months he had advanced 500 miles and captured 130,000 prisoners.

Hitler was forced, reluctantly, to come to Mussolini's aid. In February 1941, he sent a small tank force under General Erwin Rommel to Tripoli. Rommel had taken part in the blitzkrieg in France. He decided to create an illusion of strength by producing large numbers of dummy tanks, mounted on Volkswagens.

Rommel guessed that the British tanks would have been worn out by their long advance – the desert sand halved the life of a tank. In March he went on to the offensive. The British forces retreated toward Egypt. By April 11 they had lost all their Libyan gains except Tobruk, and O'Connor had been captured. Rommel wrote:

> The British had been completely deceived as to our real strength. Their moves would have been very astute if they had in fact been attacked by a force as strong as they supposed . . . At Mechili the British were taken completely by surprise and were probably again deceived as to our true strength by the dust clouds which were deliberately stirred up by our troops.[29]

Rommel had used the blitzkrieg element of surprise to mount his attack.

◀ Rommel's Afrika Korps made use of motorcycles for desert reconnaissance.

▼ As an army retreated it could concentrate its forces, while the advancing army was weakened by lengthening supply routes. Eventually, a retreating army might be strong enough to go on the offensive.

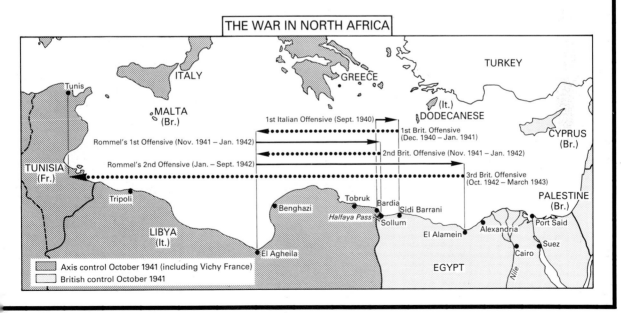

THE WAR IN NORTH AFRICA

ITALY
GREECE
TURKEY
Tunis
MALTA (Br.)
DODECANESE (It.)
CYPRUS (Br.)
TUNISIA (Fr.)
Tripoli
Benghazi
Tobruk
Bardia
Sidi Barrani
Halfaya Pass
Sollum
PALESTINE (Br.)
Port Said
LIBYA (It.)
El Alamein
Alexandria
Suez
El Agheila
Cairo
EGYPT
Nile

1st Italian Offensive (Sept. 1940)
1st Brit. Offensive (Dec. 1940 – Jan. 1941)
Rommel's 1st Offensive (Nov. 1941 – Jan. 1942)
2nd Brit. Offensive (Nov. 1941 – Jan. 1942)
Rommel's 2nd Offensive (Jan. – Sept. 1942)
3rd Brit. Offensive (Oct. 1942 – March 1943)

Axis control October 1941 (including Vichy France)
British control October 1941

Rommel – The Desert Fox

Rommel had shown the brilliance of his blitzkrieg tactics. When it was again the turn of the British to attack, he showed that he could be equally effective on the defensive.

"Operation Battleax" was an attack by 200 British tanks on the German position at Sollum. But for the first time in the war, the defenders had the advantage of surprise. Rommel used 88 mm flak (anti-aircraft) guns as anti-tank weapons. With their long range and power, they tore into the advancing tanks before they had a chance to fire back. Ninety-one British tanks were lost. Rommel restored the advantage to the defense.

A major reason for the British failure was that they were still using the rigid system of command from the rear. According to Rommel's Chief of Staff, Fritz Bayerlein, this was a serious drawback in desert war:

> *Immobility and a rigid adherence to pattern are bad enough in European warfare; in the desert they are disastrous. Here everything is in flux; there are no obstructions, no lines, water or woods for cover . . . the commander must adapt and reorientate himself daily, even hourly, and retain his freedom of action.* [30]

The British General Montgomery was a cautious commander. He would not attack unless he knew his forces were superior in number.

Rommel's understanding of the tactics necessary for desert warfare led to his great success in North Africa. He was finally defeated when the Allies cut off his supplies.

Rommel's ability to improvise, and to take advantage of every opportunity, made him the perfect blitzkrieg commander, and earned him the nickname "The Desert Fox." But it was not tactics that finally determined the outcome of the desert war, it was the problem of supply. Rommel depended on convoys of armaments and fuel sent across the Mediterranean. This was a risky route, and many ships were sunk by the British forces in Malta. Meanwhile the Allies poured reinforcements into North Africa, sending them around the Cape and through the Red Sea. Thanks to the Arabian oilfields, they also had unlimited fuel supplies.

In October 1942, Rommel was defeated at El Alamein, during a lengthy battle of attrition. The victor of El Alamein, Lieutenant-General Montgomery, did not believe in taking risks. His method was to build up massive superiority in force, which he then used in a conventional frontal assault. General von Thoma, who took part in the battle, later said:

> *Rommel realized that he had gone too far – with his limited forces and difficult supply line – but his success had caused such a sensation that he could not draw back. Hitler would not let him . . . he had to stay there until the British had gathered overwhelming forces to smash him.*[31]

Hitler would not let Rommel withdraw, so the British were able to take advantage of his weakness.

7

OPERATION BARBAROSSA
Why did Hitler attack the USSR?

IN 1940 HITLER HAD a non-aggression pact with Stalin, who was supplying vital raw materials for the German war machine – oil from the Caucasus and rubber from the east. Despite this, in December 1940, he issued a military directive for a new blitzkrieg – the USSR was to be crushed in a quick campaign codenamed "Operation Barbarossa." Years later, Guderian described his astonished reaction to this directive:

I could scarcely believe my eyes . . . Hitler had criticized the leaders of German policy of 1914 . . . for their failure to avoid a war on two fronts; was he now, on his own initiative and before the war with England had been decided, to open this second front war against the Russians? [32]

Why did Hitler now decide to launch a war on two fronts? Some historians see his decision as the logical result of his political beliefs. For twenty years he had carried out a crusade against communism and had called for German expansion eastward. But he also gave some quite different reasons. One of the most important was Britain's refusal to ask for peace:

The possibility of a Russian intervention in the war is keeping England going . . . For this reason Russia must be beaten. Then, either the English would give in or Germany would be able to continue the fight against Britain under more favourable circumstances. [33]

By "favorable circumstances," Hitler meant the seizure of the vast economic resources of the USSR and the removal of the threat of a Soviet attack. Hitler told Mussolini:

There is evident in the Soviet Union a consistent trend . . . to expand the Soviet State . . . The concentration of Russian forces is tremendous. Really, all available Russian forces are at our border. [34]

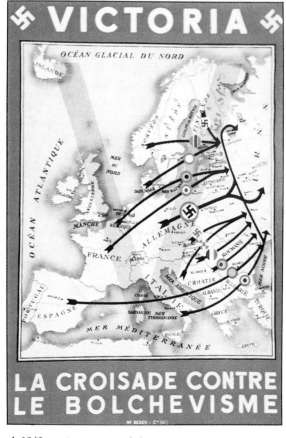

A 1942 poster presented the war against the USSR as a crusade against Bolshevism. Several European nations sent troops to fight with the German Army.

So this was to be a preventive war. Paradoxically, by beating the USSR, Hitler

A British poster, printed in Arabic, showing the uncomfortable alliance between Hitler and Stalin.

تقدمُ التعَـاونِ الألمـانى الروسـى

believed he could avoid the threat of a war on two fronts. Despite Hitler's talk of a Soviet threat, few people in 1941 thought that the Red Army could defeat Hitler. Stalin had killed his best generals; and in 1939-40, his badly-led soldiers had initially been unable to defeat the much smaller Finnish forces. Winston Churchill said that the Soviet invasion of Finland "had exposed, for the world to see, the military incapacity of the Red Army."[35] Hitler shared this view; the campaign against the Soviets would be child's play:

> We have only to kick in the door and the whole rotten structure will come crashing down.[36]

Blitzkrieg on the USSR

This cartoon that appeared in the British newspaper the *Evening Standard* on July 9, 1941, portrays British attitudes toward Operation Barbarossa.

How do you defeat a country as vast as the USSR in a lightning war? Is it possible to utilize the elements of blitzkrieg when a large area has to be covered? Hitler's solution to the problem was flawed from the start. He decided to divide his invading forces into three armies: the northern one would attack Leningrad, important for its industries; in the center, the target was the capital, Moscow; in the south, the Germans would invade the agricultural and industrial Ukraine, and then move on to the oilfields of the Caucasus.

Having divided his forces, Hitler further weakened them by reducing the number of tanks in each division. He did this to create the extra divisions he needed to cover the huge distances, but as a consequence a central idea of blitzkrieg, concentration of force, was ignored. Hitler believed he could risk spreading his forces thinly because the Red Army was an inferior force, and Stalin's regime was considered to be unpopular. General von Kleist explained:

> Hopes of victory were largely built on the prospect . . . that Stalin would be overthrown by his own people if he suffered heavy defeats . . . There were no preparations for a prolonged struggle.[37]

At first this confidence seemed justified. When Operation Barbarossa opened, on June 22, 1941, the Soviets were taken completely by surprise. Stalin refused to believe the invasion was really happening. He thought the attack was a provocation by a German commander acting independently of Hitler, and ordered his frontline soldiers not to fire back. The Soviet frontier armies were swiftly encircled or defeated. On July 3, General Halder wrote in his diary:

> It is probably no exaggeration to say that the Russian campaign has been won in the space of two weeks.[38]

But despite rapid advances, on July 6 a German newspaper report stated:

> *The mental paralysis which usually follows after the lightning German breakthroughs in the west did not occur to the same extent in the east. In most cases the enemy did not lose his capacity for action, but tried in his turn to envelop the arms of the German pincers.*[39]

On August 11, General Halder revised his earlier opinion:

> *At the outset of the war we reckoned with about 200 enemy divisions. Now we have already counted 360. . . . if we smash a dozen of them, the Russians simply put up another dozen. The time factor favors them, as they are near their own resources, whereas we are moving farther and farther away from ours.*[40]

Hitler had taken the Russians by surprise, but now his campaign lost momentum.

▲ A Soviet poster encouraging people to become partisans, or guerrillas, and fight the Germans behind the lines. Soviet partisans, fighting in conditions and territory that they knew well, were a constant problem for the regular German troops.

◄ A German tank strikes a Soviet munitions truck. The Soviets were initially unprepared for attack and easily succumbed to the highly organized German forces.

The road to Stalingrad

> *We were not prepared for what we found because our maps in no way corresponded to reality . . . all supposed roads were marked in red . . . but they often proved to be merely sandy tracks . . . Such country was bad enough for the tanks, but worse still for the transport accompanying them.*[41]

This description by General Blumentritt partly explains why Operation Barbarossa failed. Blitzkrieg depends on both surprise and speed. The second factor was particularly important in a country the size of the USSR. The Wehrmacht had to win before the harsh Russian winter, for which it was not equipped.

Heavy rains turned the primitive roads into rivers of mud, trapping the German wheeled transport and slowing the German advance. It was not till October that Guderian's panzers reached striking distance of Moscow. On October 6, sixty-five miles

The German reliance on wheeled transportation for support vehicles proved a major handicap in the invasion. Torrential rain turned the primitive Russian roads into flowing mud.

In the bitterly cold Russian winter of 1941, this German driver built an igloo around his truck to prevent the engine from freezing.

from their target, they were halted by the snow and rain of an early Russian winter. In November, freezing weather hardened the roads, but immobilized the tanks.

The Red Army had suffered major defeats, but it continued to be reinforced. Soviet armaments industries had been moved to the east, beyond the Ural mountains, where they could produce tanks and planes out of range of the German bombers. In the winter of 1941, the Red Army was strong enough to go on the offensive.

The Soviet offensive caused a crisis in the German military leadership. When the generals demanded the withdrawal of the Wehrmacht, Hitler refused and appointed himself Commander-in-Chief. Guderian, who had already started to withdraw, was fired. Hitler issued this directive:

> There must be no withdrawal . . . The enemy will gradually bleed themselves to death with their attacks.[42]

The German soldiers, still in their summer uniforms, prepared strong defensive positions. Despite huge casualties, they managed to hold on throughout the winter. In May 1942, Hitler said:

> The fact that we have survived this winter and are now in a position to go on the offensive again . . . all this is only due to the bravery of the soldiers at the front and my determined will to hold on come what may.[43]

Hitler planned to conquer Russia before another winter came upon his soliders.

The German summer offensive of 1942, aimed at Stalingrad and the oilfields of the Caucasus, was designed to cut off the Red Army's fuel supply. The battle for Stalingrad, which began on August 23, saw the hardest fighting of the war. After three months, Hitler declared, "We have got it! There are only a few places not captured."[44] But now it was the Red Army's turn to produce a surprise.

Stalingrad, Kharkov and Kursk

While the German Sixth Army was fighting its way into Stalingrad, the Russians under Marshal Zhukov massed huge reinforcements for a counter-attack. Zhukov's offensive, on November 18, took the form of two huge pincer movements encircling the German Army. When General Paulus realized what was happening, he appealed to Hitler to allow him to break out of the trap before it was too strong. Hitler refused, maintaining his "no withdrawal" strategy. As a result, the entire Sixth Army of 300,000 men was surrounded. For over two months the

Germans held out, weakened by starvation, cold and Russian shells. On February 2, Paulus and 91,000 survivors surrendered.

Hitler was forced to accept his rigid strategy had been responsible for the Stalingrad disaster. Now more open to the advice of his generals, when Field Marshal Manstein suggested using mobile defense against the Soviets, Hitler agreed, though this meant giving up captured territory. Manstein guessed the Red Army would follow up its victory at Stalingrad with a new offensive toward the Dnieper, the weakest part of the

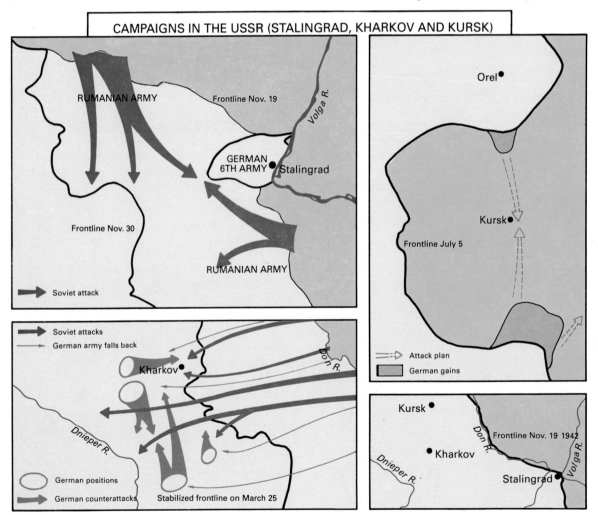

CAMPAIGNS IN THE USSR (STALINGRAD, KHARKOV AND KURSK)

A Soviet poster designed to inspire the soldiers of the Red Army. The figures in the background are the military heroes of Russia's past. This poster is particularly interesting because it appeals not to loyalty to the Communist regime but to traditional Russian patriotism.

We must be sure . . . that the advantage of surprise is maintained and . . . concentrate the attacking forces . . . to ensure . . . a massive local superiority.[45]

German front. He planned to fall back from the front line, giving the impression of a retreat. His troops would wait, in concentrated pockets, for the Russian offensive to exhaust itself. When the Soviet tanks ran out of fuel, the Germans would attack their over-extended columns.

The counter-attack around Kharkov in February 1943 was a spectacular success. By giving up territory, the Wehrmacht could concentrate its striking force and wait for the right opportunity to attack. Manstein's use of mobile defense restored the crumbling German front.

After Kharkov Hitler decided to regain the initiative with a new blitzkrieg attack on a bulge in the Soviet line at Kursk:

But the Soviets, warned by spies at German headquarters, prepared an elaborate defense system in depth. A network of mines, anti-tank guns, rocket launchers and tanks was constructed. The German attack on July 4 resulted in the largest tank battle of the whole war. After nine days, Hitler abandoned the attack. General Mellenthin wrote:

Our panzer divisions . . . had been bled white . . . With the failure of our supreme effort, the strategic initiative passed to the Russians.[46]

Had a real defense against blitzkrieg finally been found?

8

LAST YEARS OF HITLER'S GERMANY
Building a total war economy

THE FAILURE TO CONQUER the USSR had major implications for the German economy. Armaments minister, Albert Speer, wrote in his postwar autobiography:

> *Alarmed by the setbacks on the Russian front, in the spring of 1942 I considered total mobilization of all auxiliary forces . . . We had reached a turning point in our wartime economy; for until the autumn of 1941 the economic leadership had been basing its policies on short wars with long stretches of quiet in between. Now the permanent war was beginning.*[47]

Changes in German factory production now became necessary.

One other event contributed to the "permanent war." On December 11, 1941, following the Japanese attack on the American fleet at Pearl Harbor, Hitler declared war on the United States. Hitler was not bound by treaty to help the Japanese but had long resented American aid to Britain and believed that an undeclared state of war already existed between Nazi Germany and the United States.

Speer's task was to adapt a blitzkrieg economy for "total war." From the start he was frustrated by Nazi ideology and the structure of the Nazi state. Hitler found it ideologically unacceptable to conscript women for munitions work, saying "the sacrifice of our most cherished ideal is too great a price"[48]: a woman's place was in the home.

The Nazi state was governed by a number

The Japanese surprised the United States Navy with a classic blitzkrieg attack on the fleet at Pearl Harbor in December 1941. Within days, Hitler joined the Japanese in their war against the United States.

◀ Although Hitler refused to conscript women, many volunteered for war work. This 1943 painting shows women munitions workers.

▼ This graph shows the increasing proportion of German industrial production devoted to war materials such as arms and armaments.

of powerful bodies, which were almost all resistant to change. Heinrich Himmler's SS started as Hitler's personal guard, but had gradually increased its power to become almost a state within a state, engaged in building its own economic empire in the conquered territories. One of the SS's responsibilities was the systematic killing of millions of Jews in the concentration camps. At a time of "total war," Himmler was diverting German resources for the running of these camps.

Speer also had to deal with the Nazi Party's regional chiefs, or Gauleiters. According to the head of steel production, Walter Rohland, the Gauleiters resisted any attempt to transform the economy:

As a result of the brilliantly successful first two years of the war, no one believed in the necessity for total war. This was particularly true as regards the employment of labor and the reduction of consumer goods . . . the Gauleiters [thought] that the total war demanded by Speer would weaken the nation's powers of resistance.[49]

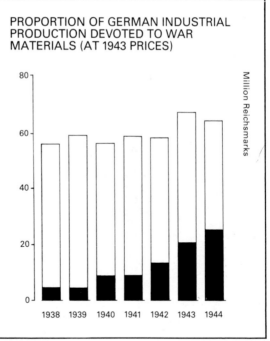

PROPORTION OF GERMAN INDUSTRIAL PRODUCTION DEVOTED TO WAR MATERIALS (AT 1943 PRICES)

Million Reichsmarks

80
60
40
20
0

1938 1939 1940 1941 1942 1943 1944

A "total war" economy would involve making unpopular sacrifices at home.

Despite this opposition, Speer succeeded in trebling armament production between 1942 and 1944 – thus prolonging the war.

Hitler and the generals

Blitzkrieg theory had always stressed leadership from the front and improvisation. But in 1943 Hitler increasingly issued detailed orders from the rear. General Heinrici said:

> Hitler always tried to make us fight for every yard, threatening to court martial anyone who didn't. No withdrawal was officially permitted without his approval . . . Time after time, forces stayed in impossible positions until they were surrounded.[50]

This is Albert Speer's explanation for Germany's defeats:

> Hitler and his military advisers thought they could lead the army from their maps. They knew nothing of the Russian winter and its road conditions . . . Hitler pushed about on the map divisions that had worn themselves out in previous fighting and . . . frequently set schedules that were completely unrealistic.[51]

Many German officers felt frustrated and angry about Hitler's conduct of the war. In 1943, a number of them reached the conclusion that the war was lost and Hitler should be removed from power. His military leadership was responsible for the disasters in the east. His political leadership had led to the Allied demands for Germany's unconditional surrender. Germany's only chance of negotiating a favorable peace lay in removing the Nazi regime.

Since before the war, a secret German resistance group had looked to the Wehrmacht as the only force powerful enough to oust Hitler. But his run of successes had prevented any effective action. The German Army's defeats of 1943 gave the conspirators their opportunity.

This is one of the last photographs of Adolf Hitler. Toward the end of the war he declined physically and became increasingly irrational. Shortly after this picture was taken, Berlin fell to the Allies and Hitler committed suicide in his bunker.

◀ This December 1941 cartoon had the caption, "In future the army will be guided by my intuitions." As he leads the dismayed German generals, Hitler wears five hats – showing the multiple roles he had taken on. Note that the right side of the picture is darker than the left.

▼ This 1944 Soviet cartoon by Kukriniksi shows a ragged German general returning from the Eastern Front to ask Hitler for orders. Hitler is shown talking through his behind.

Between 1943 and 1944, several attempts were made on Hitler's life, culminating in the bombing of his headquarters at Rastenburg in July 1944. Hitler survived with minor injuries and ruthlessly suppressed the conspiracy: a field marshal, seventeen generals and more than fifty other officers were executed.

Why were the generals unable to get rid of Hitler? The answer lies in the officer caste's code of honor. Because, in 1934, Hitler had made the army swear a personal oath of allegiance to him, some of the most important generals refused to join the conspiracy. Guderian explained:

The great proportion of the German people still believed in Adolf Hitler and would have been convinced that with his death the assassin had removed the only man who might still have been able to bring the war to a favorable conclusion . . . The people's hatred and contempt would have turned against the soldiers who, in the midst of a national struggle for existence, had broken their oath [and] murdered the head of government.[52]

D-Day

◀ One of the Allied beachheads in Normandy. In the foreground, soldiers wade through the water with their bicycles.

▼ General Dwight D. Eisenhower, the supreme commander of the Allied forces, talks to his soldiers on D-Day.

In 1943, Germany lost the initiative in the war. In the east, the Wehrmacht was in steady retreat after Kursk. In the west, it was only a matter of time before the Allies would invade occupied France. During April 1944, Hitler discussed the prospects of invasion with Mussolini:

> *When the invasion came there would be only one surprise and that would be the one the English would receive when they landed.*[53]

Hitler's optimistic view underestimated the enormous difficulties of defending the 2,000-mile French coastline – he had only 60 divisions in the west, while 200 divisions were losing the war in the east. Where should the Germans use their limited forces? Where would the Allies land?

The generals were deeply divided. Rommel believed the Wehrmacht should use all its resources "to beat off the enemy landing on the coast and to fight the battle in the . . . coastal strip."[54] Von Rundstedt described this strategy as the "tired Maginot spirit"[55] – the faith in linear defense that had been the undoing of France. He favored mobile defense – the panzers should hold back from the coast, and then mount a counter-attack against the Allies after they had landed. Rommel opposed these methods:

> *Our freedom of maneuver in the west is gone . . . The day of the dashing cut-and-thrust tank attack of the early war years is past.*[56]

Rommel knew the Allies had air superiority. Hitler decided on the worst possible solution, a compromise between the two strategies. Rommel was ordered to defend the coast, but starved of the reserves he needed.

Now that it was the Allies' turn to go on the offensive. They used the lessons they had learned from their wartime experiences.

Deception was used to make the Germans believe the landing would take place on the Calais coast – the obvious target. The real invasion, in Normandy, on D-Day, June 6, 1944, achieved complete surprise. It opened with massive aerial and naval bombardment, sabotage of communications by the French resistance and by parachutists, and the landing of 176,000 men on the Normandy beaches. Rommel's troops fought fiercely, but they were hopelessly outnumbered.

Again, Hitler's tactics contributed to the disaster. Instead of allowing Rommel to withdraw his men, he ordered a counter-offensive against the American troops driving into Brittany. This had no chance of succeeding and resulted in the death of 10,000 Germans and the capture of 50,000, encircled by the Allies in a pocket at Falaise. The way across France now lay open.

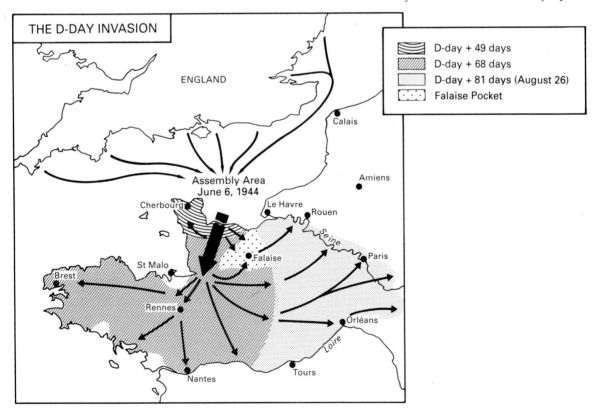

THE D-DAY INVASION

ENGLAND

D-day + 49 days
D-day + 68 days
D-day + 81 days (August 26)
Falaise Pocket

Calais

Amiens

Assembly Area
June 6, 1944

Cherbourg
Le Havre
Rouen
Seine
Paris

St Malo
Falaise

Brest

Rennes
Orléans

Nantes
Tours
Loire

Hitler's last blitzkrieg

Throughout the second half of 1944, Germany was gradually forced to relinquish its European conquests. By September, the western Allies had driven into Belgium, but lengthening supply lines slowed their advance. As the Wehrmacht retreated, it was able to concentrate its forces until, on the German borders, it stood in a strong defensive position.

Hitler knew it was hopeless to fight a defensive war on two fronts. He decided a surprise attack in the Ardennes could split the invading armies in two and cut the supply lines of those in the north. As in 1940, the Ardennes were thinly defended – the Germans could repeat "Operation Sicklecut."

But the Wehrmacht was in no position to mount an offensive. To gather enough troops, the call-up age was reduced to sixteen, and convicted criminals and the sick were conscripted. The overwhelming air superiority of the Allies meant the attack must take place in bad weather, when the planes would be grounded. General Josef Dietrich, in charge of the Sixth SS Panzer Army, complained:

> *All Hitler wants me to do is to cross a river, capture Brussels, and then go on and take Antwerp! And all this in the worst time of year through the Ardennes where the snow is waist deep and there isn't room to deploy four tanks abreast let alone armored divisions! Where it doesn't get light until eight and it's dark again at four and with re-formed divisions made up chiefly of kids and sick old men – and at Christmas!*[57]

The plan was absurd, but for that reason it came as a complete surprise. In the early hours of December 16, 1944, the offensive opened under the cover of fog. Four American infantry divisions were attacked by twenty German divisions. Units of English-speaking Germans, dressed in U.S. Army uniforms, appeared behind the lines, moving road signs, cutting telephone wires

American soldiers during the Ardennes offensive. The bad weather made fighting difficult for Germans and Americans alike.

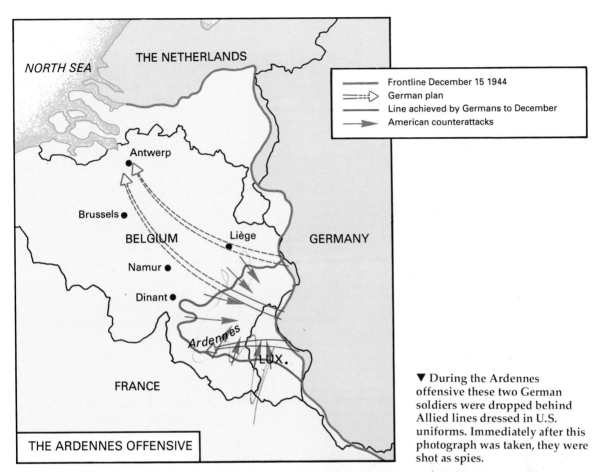

THE NETHERLANDS

NORTH SEA

Frontline December 15 1944
German plan
Line achieved by Germans to December
American counterattacks

Antwerp

Brussels

BELGIUM

Liège

GERMANY

Namur

Dinant

Ardennes

LUX.

FRANCE

THE ARDENNES OFFENSIVE

▼ During the Ardennes
offensive these two German
soldiers were dropped behind
Allied lines dressed in U.S.
uniforms. Immediately after this
photograph was taken, they were
shot as spies.

and causing confusion.

But the Americans put up a strong defense, delaying the German attack while reinforcements were rushed to the area. The German offensive was doomed by lack of fuel and reserves. When the weather improved on December 23, the Allies exploited their air superiority in a strong counter-attack. Field Marshal von Rundstedt later recalled:

Each step forward in the Ardennes offensive prolonged our flanks more dangerously deep, making them more susceptible to Allied counter-strokes. I wanted to stop the offensive at an early stage, when it was plain that it could not achieve its aim, but Hitler furiously insisted that it must go on.[58]

Defeat

Germans walking through the bombed streets of Koblenz in March 1945. They had been asked to leave their homes by the advancing Allied troops who were concerned about sniper fire.

Hitler's gamble in the Ardennes failed, not just because of scarce resources but also because the Allies understood the blitzkrieg technique. General Patton knew deep penetration by the Germans would weaken their flanks. He said:

> *Let the bastards go all the way to Paris; then we can cut them up and chew them off.*[59]

Patton's words illustrate the differences between 1940 and 1944. Blitzkrieg worked in 1940 because it was a new method of fighting that swiftly demoralized its opponents. But in 1944, the Allies identified the direction of the German attack and waited for the Wehrmacht to exhaust its supplies before counter-attacking. B. H. Liddell Hart, the military historian, wrote:

> *The Ardennes offensive carried to the extreme of absurdity the military belief that "attack is the best defense." It proved the "worst defense" wrecking Germany's chance of any further serious resistance.*[60]

When the Soviets launched a major new offensive on January 12, the Wehrmacht had no reserves left to use against them. Despite this hopeless position, it took four more months of fighting to make Germany surrender. Liddell Hart, who interviewed the German generals in prison after the war, put forward this explanation:

> All to whom I talked dwelt on the effect of the Allies' "unconditional surrender" policy in prolonging the war. They told me that but for this they and their troops – the factor that was more important – would have been ready to surrender sooner . . . Allied propaganda never said anything positive about the peace conditions in the way of encouraging them to give up the struggle. [61]

A factor that certainly prolonged the fighting was Hitler's refusal to admit the war was lost. Until the end he issued orders to non-existent armies from his bunker in Berlin. On April 30, 1945, when Berlin fell to the Red Army, Hitler shot himself. Before his suicide, he wrote a "Political Testament," in which he laid the blame for Germany's defeat with "international Jewry" and denounced the German generals. It concluded:

> The efforts and sacrifices of the German people in this war have been so great that I cannot believe that they have been in vain. The aim must still be to win territory in the east for the German people. [62]

This statement reveals the extent of Hitler's grasp of reality.

A week later the German High Command had accepted the Allies' demand for unconditional surrender.

▲ Bodies of dead German civilians, laid out for identification. They were the victims of an Allied bombing raid.

◄ March 1945. Civilians in a captured German town unload a radio set in compliance with military orders to surrender radio sets.

CONCLUSION
The technological war

BETWEEN 1939 AND 1941, the blitzkrieg method revolutionized warfare and gave Germany a series of swift easy victories. But in 1942, Hitler's lightning war turned into a war of attrition, the limited war into a world war. Part of the reason for this lies with Hitler's strategic mistakes. Instead of concentrating his forces, he spread them out and attacked too many enemies at once. Instead of allowing his generals to improvise and use mobility in defense, Hitler increasingly issued orders from the rear and insisted on rigid defensive strategies.

Blitzkrieg also failed because it depended for its success on surprise. As its novelty decreased, so did its effectiveness. The Allies were able to develop strategies to rob it of its power, such as the use of defense in depth.

The history of warfare is about a constant search for novelty, in technology as well as in tactics. In January 1942, Hitler said:

> *Tanks will have finished their career before the end of this war . . . Necessity teaches men . . . ceaselessly to invent, and above all to accept the inventions that are suggested to them. Every new suggestion so much reduces the value of the previous material that it's a ceaselessly renewed struggle to introduce a novelty.*[63]

This photograph of Hiroshima, taken some time after the dropping of the atomic bomb, shows the extent of the devastation.

◀ The German V-2 rocket was one of the secret weapons on which Hitler increasingly pinned his hopes of victory. However, the V-weapons were developed too late to change the course of the war.

▼ The radar receiving-room on a U.S. aircraft carrier. A technician logs the information received by radio waves on a transparent screen.

Although tanks had not finished their career by 1945, they had to be constantly improved to maintain their effectiveness. Such technological development to a large extent determined the course of the war. For example, the British Air Force owed its success in the Battle of Britain largely to the use of radar – a method of detecting enemy planes at long range using radio waves.

The Allies used the same principle in the development of the proximity fuse – a radio transmitter and receiver fitted into the nose of a shell. Radio waves caused the shell to explode at the right distance from its target to cause the most damage. This technology became a major factor in defeating the Japanese Air Force over the Pacific.

The ultimate development of this technological war was the atomic bomb, dropped on Hiroshima and Nagasaki in August 1945. In 1938, two German scientists had discovered a new way of splitting the uranium atom, a process that in theory could release enormous energy. However,

German nuclear research was years behind that of the Allies, and it was the United States that developed and used the atomic bomb. Since 1945, with the continuing development of weapons, blitzkrieg is now seen as a "conventional" method of warfare.

Leading figures

Heinz Guderian (1888–1954)
German general
Heinz Guderian created Germany's panzer divisions, and contributed more than any other general to the development of blitzkrieg. Guderian led from the front, commanding panzer spearheads in the invasions of Poland and France. In France, he organized the breakthrough at Sedan, and in 1941 he was in charge of the panzer forces advancing on Moscow. During the December Soviet offensive, he ordered a withdrawal against Hitler's wishes and was dismissed. He was not given another command until February 1943 – his task was to rebuild the panzer forces after the Stalingrad disaster. In July 1944 he was made Chief of the General Staff. The following March, when he told Hitler that the war was lost, Guderian was dismissed for the last time.

Adolf Hitler (1889–1945)
Führer (leader) of Germany
After four years as a soldier in World War I, Hitler joined the tiny right-wing German Workers' Party in 1919. He quickly dominated it; in 1921 he became leader of the party – renamed the National Socialist German Workers' Party (Nazi Party). In 1923 he led the Nazis' unsuccessful attempt to seize power. During his subsequent imprisonment, Hitler wrote *Mein Kampf* (My Struggle), in which he described his vision of Germany's future: military conquests in the east to provide living space for the "German race." After becoming Chancellor in 1933, Hitler outlawed all other political parties and

Hitler, German Führer, and Mussolini, Dictator of Italy, acknowledging the cheers of a German crowd. Hitler was the dominant figure in their alliance.

This photograph of Montgomery was taken in northern France shortly after the D-Day landings. He called his pet dogs Hitler and Rommel!

declared himself Führer. During World War II, he played an increasingly dominant role in military strategy, appointing himself Commander-in-Chief in 1941. In April 1945, when the Red Army was storming Berlin, Hitler committed suicide.

Erich von Manstein (1887–1973)
German field marshal
Manstein was the Wehrmacht's greatest military strategist. In 1940, he developed the plan for the invasion of France. Although his plan was adopted, he made enemies in the High Command and was only given the command of an infantry corps during the actual invasion. When Germany attacked the USSR, Manstein's panzer corps advanced two hundred miles in four days. After organizing the conquest of the Crimea, he was given the impossible task of relieving the German Army trapped at Stalingrad. Although he failed, his use of mobile defense at Kharkov saved the Eastern Front. After the Soviet victories of 1943, Manstein argued that the Wehrmacht should make a long tactical

withdrawal to regroup its forces. Hitler insisted that the army fight for every yard of ground, and fired Manstein in March 1944.

Sir Bernard Montgomery (1887–1976)
British general (later field marshal)
In August 1942, Montgomery was given command of the Eighth Army in North Africa. His arrival at El Alamein, the British defensive position, changed the character of the conflict from a war of maneuver to one of attrition. He slowly built up his forces until he was sure of success, before launching his attack. After this decisive victory over Rommel, Montgomery slowly pursued the Afrika Korps back to Tunisia. In September 1943, Montgomery led the Eighth Army in the invasion of Italy, advancing up the east coast to Pescara. Then he was recalled to Britain to take command of the Twenty-first Army Group in the invasion of northern Europe. Montgomery was famous for his lack of modesty; asked to name the three greatest generals of all time, he replied that the other two were Napoleon and Alexander the Great.

Erwin Rommel (1891–1944)
German field marshal

In 1940, Rommel commanded a panzer division, taking part in the crossing of the Meuse and the drive to the French coast. The following year, Hitler sent him to North Africa to help the Italians, then in full retreat. With limited forces, Rommel went on to the offensive and drove the British out of Cyrenaica. His tactics over the next eighteen months made him a national hero, but he was finally defeated at the Battle of El Alamein in October 1942. In 1944, Rommel was sent to the Channel coast to prepare for the expected Allied invasion. On July 17, he was badly injured when Allied planes fired on his car. Three days later a group of German officers tried to kill Hitler. Implicated in the plot, Rommel was eventually forced to commit suicide by taking poison.

Joseph Stalin (1879–1953) Soviet leader

Joseph Djugashvili, who renamed himself Stalin ("man of steel"), was not a Russian but a Georgian. He played a relatively minor role in the 1917 Revolution, but in the 1920s he used his position as General Secretary of the Communist Party to concentrate power in his own hands. By 1929, he had defeated all other rivals for the leadership. He then set about the rapid modernization of the USSR, forcing the peasantry to join collective farms and organizing crash-industrialization. Stalin trusted nobody and maintained power by ruthless repression. Millions of potential opponents were either shot or sent to labor camps. At the same time, he encouraged a cult of his own personality – for twenty years, he was worshiped as the wise father of his people. Stalin was hailed in the USSR as the man who won the war.

Erwin Rommel's success in desert warfare gave him a heroic reputation.

Marshal Zhukov received Germany's unconditional surrender in Berlin on May 8, 1945.

Georgi Zhukov (1896–1974) Soviet general

Zhukov was Stalin's favorite general, and on a number of occasions he was sent to rescue desperate positions. In October 1941, he was made Commander of the Central Front and was responsible for halting the German advance that threatened Moscow. In 1942 he was given the command of the southern armies and organized the encirclement of the German Army at Stalingrad. From 1944, he led the Red Army as it drove the Germans out of Poland, capturing Warsaw in January 1945. He planned the final assault on Berlin, where he received the German surrender in May. Zhukov had a reputation for ruthlessness: he told U.S. General Eisenhower that the best way to clear a minefield was to send the infantry across it.

Important dates

Date	Events
1914	
–18	World War I.
1919	*June* Treaty of Versailles.
1923	*January* French troops occupy the Ruhr.
1933	*January* Hitler appointed Chancellor of Germany.
	March The Reichstag – the German parliament – gives Hitler emergency powers.
	June/July All political parties except the Nazi Party are banned.
1934	*August* All members of the German armed forces swear an oath of loyalty to Hitler.
1935	*March* Germany reintroduces military conscription.
1936	*March* German troops enter demilitarized Rhineland.
	October Rome-Berlin axis formed.
1938	*March* Anschluss with Austria.
	September Munich agreement gives Germany the Sudetenland – the part of Czechoslovakia inhabited by Germans.
1939	*March* Germany occupies Bohemia and Moravia, the Czech area of Czechoslovakia.
	August Nazi-Soviet Pact.
	September 1 Germany invades Poland.
	September 3 Britain and France declare war on Germany.
	September 17 Soviet forces invade eastern Poland.
	October 6 Last Polish forces surrender.
	November 30 USSR invades Finland.
1940	*April 9* Germany invades Denmark and Norway.
	May 10 Germany launches attack on France, Belgium and the Netherlands.
	May 27–June 4 Allied soldiers evacuated from Dunkirk.
	June 10 Italy enters the war as Germany's ally.
	June 22 France signs armistice.
	July 10 The Battle of Britain begins.
	September 7 Beginning of the Blitz, the night bombing campaign on Britain's cities.
	September Italians invade Egypt.
	December British offensive in North Africa.
1941	*February* Rommel and the Afrika Korps arrive in Tripoli.
	April Germany invades Greece and Yugoslavia; Rommel's first offensive in North Africa.
	May German airborne invasion of Crete.
	June German invasion of the USSR; Operation Battleax – British offensive in North Africa – fails.
	December Successful British offensive in North Africa; German Army stopped at Moscow; Soviet winter offensive begins.
	December 7 Japanese attack U.S. fleet at Pearl Harbor.
	December 11 Hitler declares war on the United States.
1942	*January–June* Rommel's second offensive in North Africa.
	May German summer offensive in the USSR aimed at Stalingrad.
	October Rommel's forces defeated at the Battle of El Alamein.
	November Soviets encircle German forces attacking Stalingrad; British offensive in North Africa drives Germans out of Libya.

Date	Events

Date   **Events**

1943   *February* Surrender of the German Sixth Army at Stalingrad; Soviet offensive; German counter-offensive around Kharkov.
July Battle of Kursk; Allied invasion of Sicily.
September Allies land in Italy; Italy signs armistice.

1944   *June 6* D-Day: Allies land in Normandy.
December Hitler's last blitzkrieg, in the Ardennes – the Battle of the Bulge.

1945   *January* New Soviet offensive.
April 30 Hitler commits suicide.
May 8 Germany surrenders.
August 6 Atomic bomb dropped on Hiroshima.
August 9 Atomic bomb dropped on Nagasaki.
August 15 Japan surrenders.

Glossary

Allies	Countries that have made an agreement to further their common interests. Specifically refers to the countries fighting against Germany in both World Wars.
Anschluss	Union – in particular that of Germany and Austria in March 1938.
Appeasement	Giving in to a potential aggressor's demands to prevent war – the policy of Britain and France in 1936-9.
Armistice	A truce; the agreement to stop fighting.
Attrition	Gradual wearing out. Warfare of attrition is one in which victory goes to the side that can last the longest.
Authoritarian	Favoring obedience to government over individual liberty.
Axis	Name given to Germany and its allies – derives from an imaginary line drawn from Berlin to Rome, "the Rome-Berlin Axis."
Battle of Britain	The battle between the German and British air forces over England, July–October 1940.
Battle of the Bulge	U.S. term for Hitler's 1944 offensive in the Ardennes.
BEF	British Expeditionary Force: the British Army sent to France in 1939.
Blitz	German night bombing campaign of Britain's cities, September 1940–May 1941.
Bolsheviks	Members of the Russian Communist Party who seized power in October 1917.
Capitalism	Economic system based on free enterprise and private ownership.
Chancellor	The German chief minister, or premier.
Communism	Economic system based on common ownership of property and the creation of a classless society.
Concentration camps	Camps set up by the Nazis to imprison their opponents. During the course of the war, some of these camps became extermination camps, for the killing of Jews, gypsies, homosexuals and others.
D-Day	Name for the day of the Allied invasion of Europe, June 6, 1944.
Defense in depth	Use of multiple lines of defense, one behind the other, to prevent a breakthrough by an attacking army.
Demilitarize	To remove armed forces from an area, as in the case of the Rhineland in 1919–36.
Democracy	System in which a government is accountable to the people, who can remove it through elections.
Flank	The right or left side of an army.
Front	The foremost line of an army facing the enemy, or the scene of fighting.
League of Nations	International body set up by the Treaty of Versailles to prevent war.
Luftwaffe	The German Air Force.
Maginot Line	System of fortifications built along the Franco-German border by the French, 1930–5.
Mobile defense	System of defense in which an army gives up ground in the face of an attacking army, in order to counter-attack later.
Mobility	The ability of armed forces to move freely in battle.
Nazi Party	The National Socialist German Workers Party, led by Adolf Hitler.

Non-aggression pact	Agreement between two countries not to go to war, specifically that between Germany and the USSR in 1939.
Operation Barbarossa	Code name of the German attack on the USSR in 1941.
Operation Sicklecut	Code name for the German attack on France through the Ardennes, May 1940.
Panzer	Literally "armor," the German word for tank.
Pincers	Movement in which two or more attacking armies converge on an enemy position.
Propaganda	Spreading ideas or information to persuade or convert others.
Purge	The removal of opponents. It specifically refers to Stalin's elimination of potential enemies in the 1930s.
Radar	From "**ra**dio **d**etection **a**nd **r**anging." A method of locating objects, such as planes or ships, by sending out radio waves, which they reflect.
Reparations	Payment made by a defeated country to compensate for damage caused during a war.
SS	*Schutzstaft* – "guard detachment." Originally Hitler's bodyguard, later an élite armed force.
Strategy	The technique of managing armed forces in a campaign, or an overall plan of action.
Stuka	*Sturzkampfflugzeug* – "dive attack plane." A plane that, by dive-bombing, could achieve greater accuracy in hitting its target.
Tactics	Like strategy, the technique of managing armed forces. More specifically, the managing of armed forces in actual contact with an enemy.
Total war	Situation in which a country directs all its resources to the war effort.
Wehrmacht	The German armed forces.

Further reading

Secondary Sources

Horne, Alistair, *To Lose a Battle: France 1940*, Penguin, 1979.
Liddel Hart, B.H., *History of the Second World War*, Putnam Pub, 1980.
Strawson, John, El Alamein: *Desert Victory*, Biblio Dist. 1981.

Primary Sources

Guderion, Heinz, *Panzer Leader*, Ballantine, 1976.
Khrushchev, Nikita, *Khrushchev Remembers*, Sphere, 1971.
Liddel Hart, Basil H. (ed), *The Rommel Papers*, Da Capo, 1982.
Speer, Albert, *Inside the Third Reich*, Macmillan, 1981.
Von Mellenthin, F.W., *Panzer Battles*, Alfred Knopf, 1955.

Notes on sources

1 Guderian, H., *Panzer Leader*, Michael Joseph, 1952, p. 41.
2 Quoted in Liddell Hart, B.H., *The Other Side of the Hill*, Pan, 1978, p. 127.
3 Mellenthin, F.W. von, *Panzer Battles*, University of Oklahoma Press, 1956, p. 55.
4 Quoted in Liddell Hart, *op. cit.*, p. 29.
5 Guderian, *op. cit.*, p. 30.
6 Quoted by Sheffield, G.D., "Blitzkrieg and Attrition," MacInnes, C. and Sheffield, G.D. (eds.), *Warfare in the Twentieth Century*, Unwin Hyman, London 1988, p. 65.
7 Quoted in Shirer, W., *The Collapse of the Third Republic*, Heinemann, 1970, p. 156.
8 Quoted in Erickson, J., *The Road to Stalingrad*, Weidenfeld and Nicolson, 1975, p. 5.
9 Quoted in Strawson, J., *Hitler as Military Commander*, Sphere, 1973.
10 Quoted in *ibid.*, p. 61.
11 Quoted in Noakes, J. and Pridham, G. (eds.), *Nazism 1919–1945 Vol. 3*, Exeter Studies in History, 1988, p. 725.
12 Hitler, Adolf, *Mein Kampf*, Hutchinson, 1969, p.598.
13 Quoted in Noakes, J. and Pridham, G. (eds.), *Documents on Nazism*, Cape, 1974, p. 405.
14 Quoted in *ibid.*, p. 415.
15 Quoted in Strawson, *op. cit.*, p. 82.
16 Quoted in Shirer, *op. cit.*, p. 505.
17 Quoted in Horne, Alistair, *To Lose a Battle: France 1940*, Penguin, 1979, p. 143.
18 Quoted in Shirer, *op. cit.*, p. 511.
19 Quoted in Horne, *op. cit.*, p. 143.
20 Maurois, André, *Why France Fell*, Bodley Head, 1941, p. 41.
21 Quoted in *Nazism 1919–45 Vol.3*, p. 722.
22 Maurois, *op. cit.*, p. 102.
23 Quoted in Miksche, F.O., *Blitzkrieg*, Faber, 1941, p. 23.
24 Quoted in Liddell Hart, *op. cit.*, p. 200.
25 Quoted in Fuller, J.F.C., *The Second World War*, Eyre and Spottiswoode, 1948, p. 39.
26 Speer, Albert, *Inside the Third Reich*, Sphere, 1970, p. 300.
27 Quoted in *Nazism 1919–45 Vol.3*, p. 904.
28 Quoted in *ibid.*, p. 908.
29 Liddell Hart, B.H. (ed.), *The Rommel Papers*, Collins, 1953, p. 120.
30 *Ibid.*, p. 184.
31 Liddell Hart, *op. cit.*, p. 244.
32 Guderian, *op. cit.*, p. 142.
33 Quoted in *Nazism 1919–45 Vol. 3*, p. 813.
34 Quoted in *ibid.*, p. 816.
35 Quoted in Liddell Hart, B.H., *History of the Second World War*, Pan, 1974, p. 49.
36 Quoted in Strawson, *op. cit.*, p. 132.
37 Quoted in Liddell Hart, *The Other Side of the Hill*, p. 259.
38 Quoted in *Nazism 1919–45 Vol. 3*, p. 818.
39 Quoted in Fuller, *op. cit.*, p. 120.
40 Quoted in *Nazism 1919–45 Vol. 3*, p. 820.
41 Quoted in Liddell Hart, *The Other Side of the Hill*, p. 271.
42 Quoted in *Nazism 1919–45 Vol. 3*, p. 828.
43 Quoted in *ibid.*, p. 829.
44 Quoted in *ibid.*, p. 842.
45 Quoted in *ibid.*, p. 862.
46 Quoted in Mellenthin, *op. cit.*, p. 230.
47 Speer, Albert, *op. cit.*, p. 301.
48 Quoted in Shirer, W.L., *The Rise and Fall of the Third Reich*, Pan, 1960, p. 1291.
49 Quoted in *Documents on Nazism*, p. 653.
50 Quoted in Liddell Hart, *The Other Side of the Hill*, p. 325.
51 Speer, *op. cit.*, p. 415.
52 Guderian, *op. cit.*, p. 349.
53 Quoted in *Nazism 1919–45 Vol. 3*, p. 869-70.
54 *The Rommel Papers*, p. 455.
55 Quoted in Strawson, *op. cit.*, p. 186.
56 *The Rommel Papers*, p. 468.
57 Quoted in Hastings, Max, *Victory in Europe*, Weidenfeld and Nicolson, 1985, p. 101.
58 Quoted in Liddell Hart, *The Other Side of the Hill*, p. 464.
59 Quoted in Perrett, B., *A History of Blitzkrieg*, Stein and Day, 1983, p. 215.
60 Liddell Hart, *The Other Side of the Hill*, p. 465.
61 *Ibid.*
62 Quoted in Shirer, W.L., *The Rise and Fall of the Third Reich*, p. 1343.
63 Cameron, N. and Stevens, R.H. (trans.), *Hitler's Table Talk*, Weidenfeld and Nicolson, 1953, p. 177.

Index

Figures in **bold** refer to illustrations

Picture acknowledgments

The author and publishers would like to thank the following for allowing their illustrations to be used in this book: E.T. Archive *cover*, 41 (top); Imperial War Museum 4, 5 (top & bottom), 16, 20, 24, 33, 35 (left), 37, 44 (top & bottom), 46, 47 (bottom), 49 (top), 52, 53; Peter Newark's Military Pictures 27, 32, 43 (bottom); Popperfoto 9, 12, 17, 18, 25, 30, 42, 50, 51 (top), 55; Solo Syndication 28, 34, 43 (top); Topham 6, 7, 10, 11, 21, 26, 29 (top), 31, 35 (right), 36, 39, 40, 48, 49 (bottom), 51 (bottom), 54; Wayland Picture Library 14; Weimar Archive 13, 19, 22 (right). The artwork was supplied by Andras Bereznay.